ChordTime® Piano

Kids' Songs

Level 2B

I-IV-V⁷ chords in keys of C, G and F

This book belongs to: _____

Arranged by

Nancy and Randall Faber

Production Coordinator: Jon Ophoff
Design and Illustration: Terpstra Design, San Francisco
Engraving: Dovetree Productions, Inc.

FABER
PIANO ADVENTURES®
3042 Creek Drive
Ann Arbor, Michigan 48108

A NOTE TO TEACHERS

ChordTime® Piano Kids' Songs is a collection of popular songs that brings special enjoyment to children. The sense of fantasy and humor of the selections will motivate students to play while they learn basic harmony.

As the title **ChordTime®** suggests, the emphasis of this book is on the student's mastery of I, IV, and V^7 chords. The pieces are arranged in the keys of C, G, and F with warm-up exercises for each key. Different accompanying styles have been chosen to expand the student's recognition and application of these chords.

ChordTime® Piano Kids' Songs is part of the *ChordTime® Piano* series. "ChordTime" designates Level 2B of the *PreTime® to BigTime® Piano Supplementary Library* arranged by Faber and Faber.

Following are the levels of the supplementary library, which lead from *PreTime®* to *BigTime®*.

PreTime® Piano	(Primer Level)
PlayTime® Piano	(Level 1)
ShowTime® Piano	(Level 2A)
ChordTime® Piano	(Level 2B)
FunTime® Piano	(Level 3A – 3B)
BigTime® Piano	(Level 4)

Each level offers books in a variety of styles, making it possible for the teacher to offer stimulating material for every student. For a complimentary detailed listing, e-mail faber@pianoadventures.com or write us at the mailing address below.

Visit **www.PianoAdventures.com**.

Helpful Hints:

1. The chord warm-ups for a given key should be played daily before practicing the songs.

2. The student can be asked to identify the I, IV, and V^7 chords in each song and write the correct chord symbol below the bass staff.

3. Hands-alone practice is recommended to facilitate correct fingering and accurate rhythm.

ISBN 978-1-61677-041-9

TABLE OF CONTENTS

Key of C

C Scale Warm-up: Play **H.A.** (Hands Alone), then **H.T.** (Hands Together).

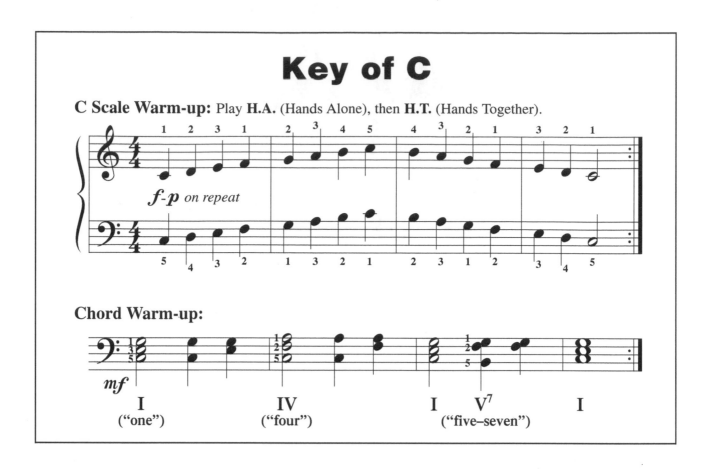

Chord Warm-up:

I ("one")   IV ("four")   I   V⁷ ("five–seven")   I

In a Cabin in the Woods

The key signature for C major
has no sharps or flats.

Moderately fast

ENGLISH

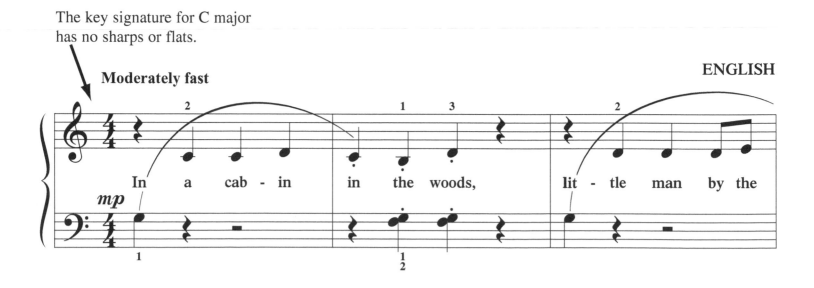

In a cab - in   in the woods,   lit - tle man by the

Mama Paquita

Key of ___ major

Traditional Song from Brazil
English words by MARGARET MARKS

8

Catch a Falling Star

Key of ___ major

Words and Music by
PAUL J. VANCE and LEE POCKRISS

Gently moving

night. And just in case you feel you want to hold her,

you'll have a pock-et full of star - light. Catch a fall-ing star and

put it in your pock - et, nev - er let it fade a - way.

Catch a fall-ing star and put it in your pock-et, save it for a rain - y day.

Ding-Dong! The Witch Is Dead

from *The Wizard Of Oz*

Key of ___ major

Lyric by E.Y. HARBURG
Music by HAROLD ARLEN

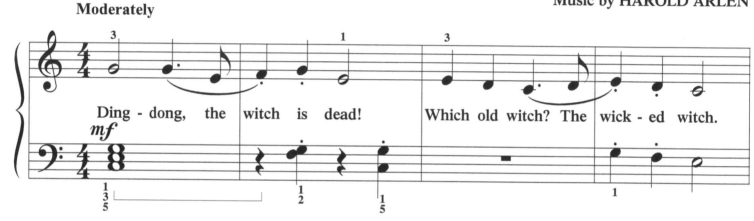

Ding - dong, the witch is dead! Which old witch? The wick - ed witch.

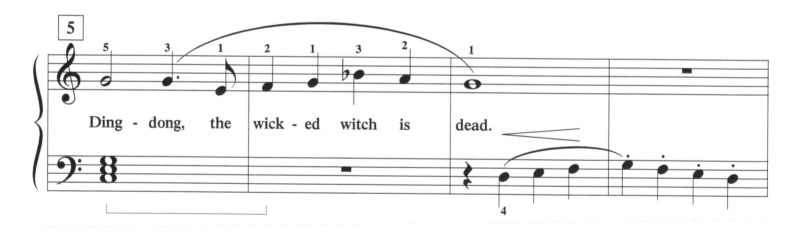

Ding - dong, the wick - ed witch is dead.

Wake up, you sleep - y head, rub your eyes, get out of bed.

Rubber Duckie

from the Television Series *Sesame Street*

Key of ___ major

Words and Music by
JEFF MOSS

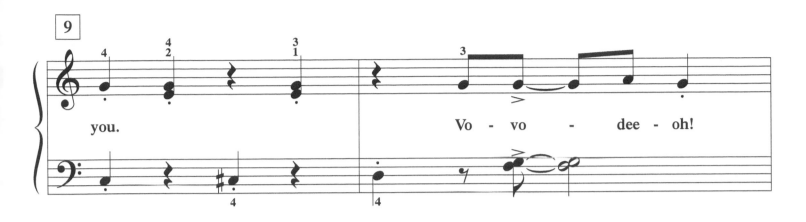

you.   Vo - vo - dee - oh!

Rub - ber Duck - ie,   you're   so   fine,____

and I'm luck-y____   that you're mine.____   Rub-ber Duck-ie, I'm

cross over

aw - ful - ly   fond   of   you!

Key of G

G Scale Warm-up: Play **H.A.** (Hands Alone), then **H.T.** (Hands Together).

Chord Warm-up:

New River Train

The key signature for G major has one sharp.

Lively

GOSPEL

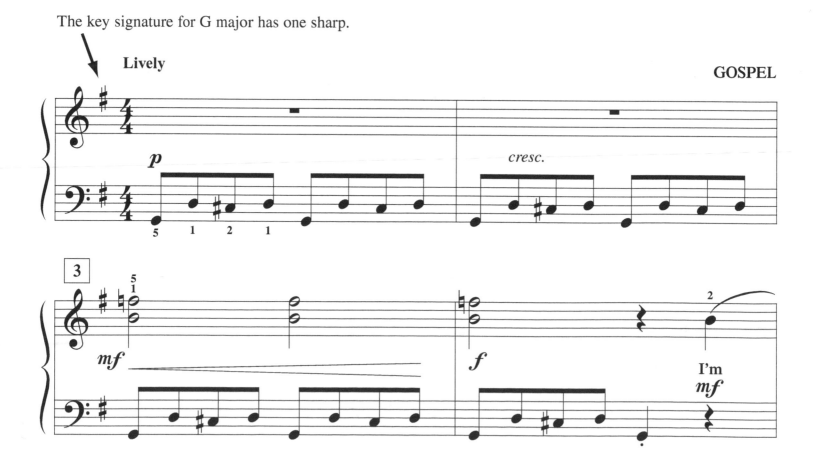

Pizza Time!

Key of ___ major

Lyric by CRYSTAL BOWMAN
Music by NANCY FABER

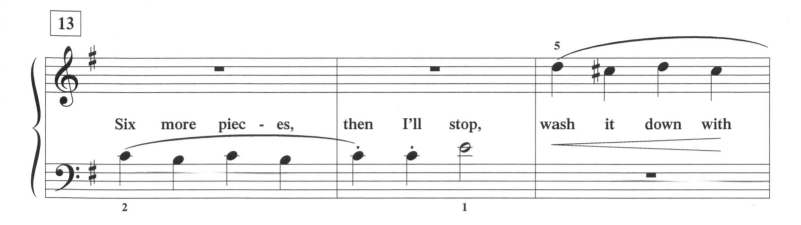

Six more piec - es, then I'll stop, wash it down with

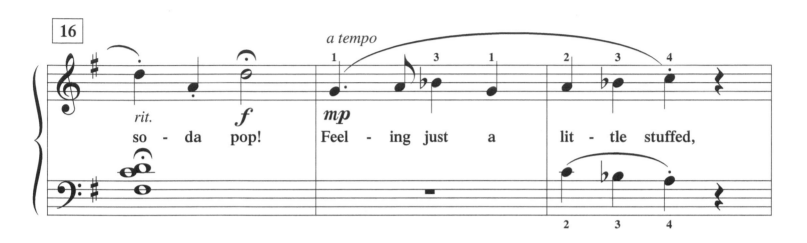

rit. *f* *a tempo* *mp*

so - da pop! Feel - ing just a lit - tle stuffed,

think that I have had e-nough. Pep - per - o - ni, sauce, and cheese,

f *mp* *ritardando*

Slow and heavy

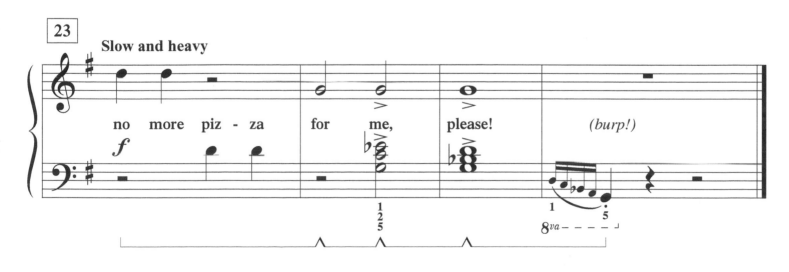

no more piz - za for me, please! (burp!)

f

8va- - - - -

Tingalayo

Key of ___ major

JAMAICAN CALYPSO SONG

Happy Birthday to You

Key of ___ major

Words and Music by
MILDRED J. HILL and PATTY S. HILL

Moderately

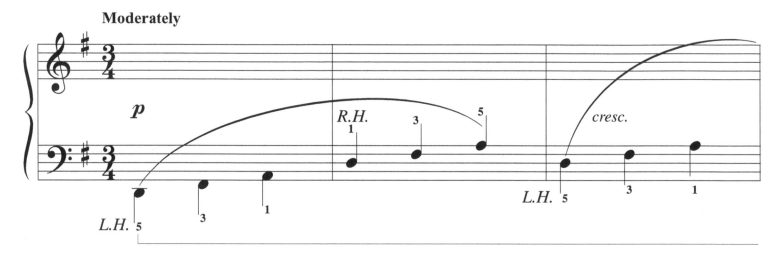

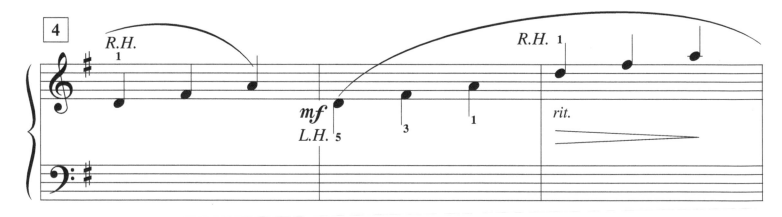

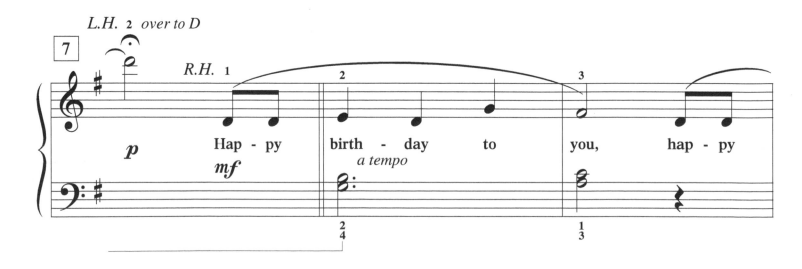

10

birth - day to you. Hap - py birth - day, dear

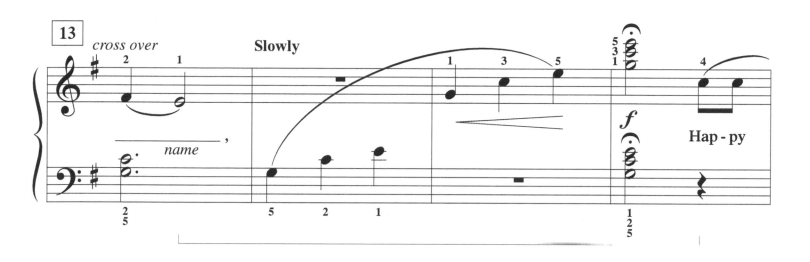

13

cross over   Slowly

name,   Hap - py

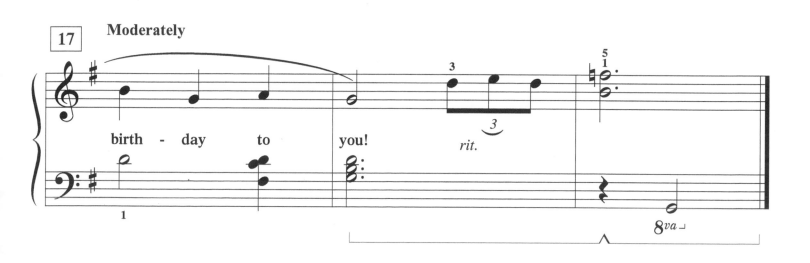

17 **Moderately**

birth - day to you!   *rit.*

Key of F

F Scale Warm-up: Play **H.A.** (Hands Alone), then **H.T.** (Hands Together).

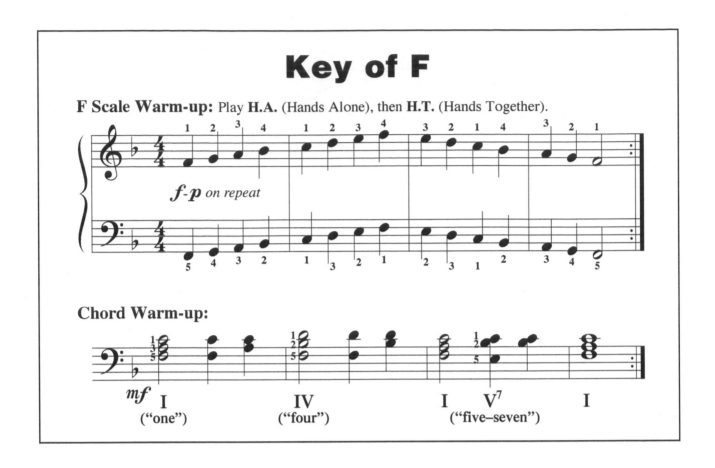

Chord Warm-up:

I Can't Spell Hippopotamus

The key signature for F major has one flat.

Brightly, with a swing

Words and Music by
J. FRED COOTS

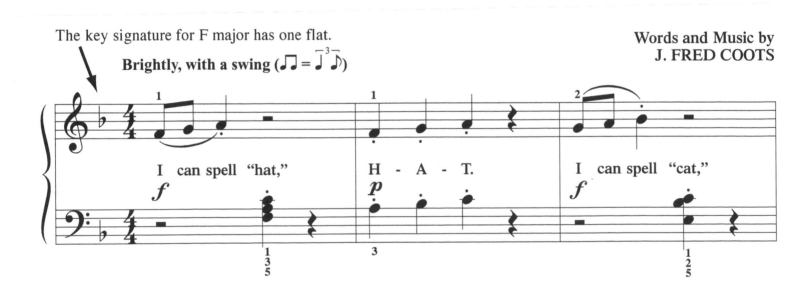

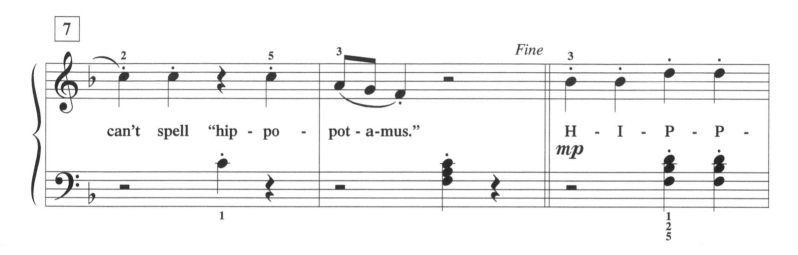

Oh! Susanna

Key of ___ major

Words and Music by
STEPHEN FOSTER

Lively

Oh, I come from Al - a - bam - a with my ban - jo on my

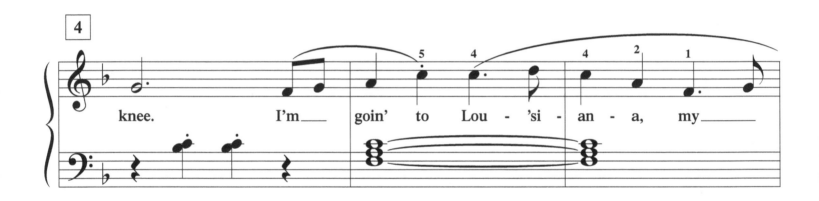

knee. I'm___ goin' to Lou - 'si - an - a, my___

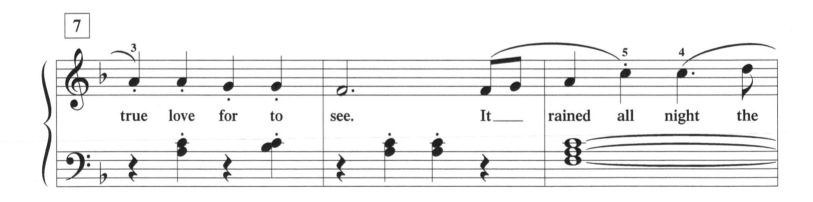

true love for to see. It___ rained all night the

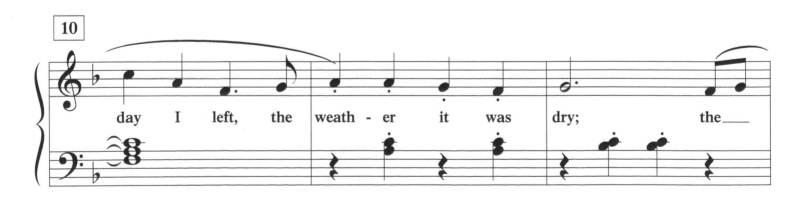

day I left, the weath - er it was dry; the___

13

sun so hot I froze to death, Su - san - na, don't you

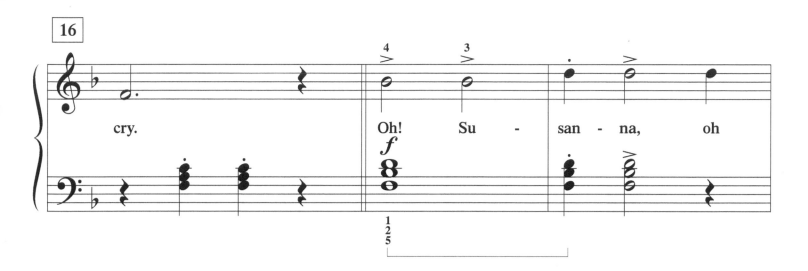

16

cry. Oh! Su - san - na, oh

19

don't you cry for me; for I come from Al - a -

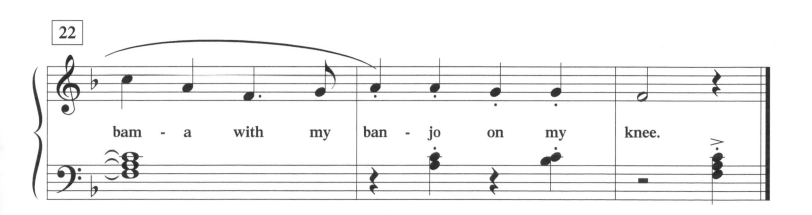

22

bam - a with my ban - jo on my knee.

The Teddy Bears' Picnic

Key of ___ major

Words by JIMMY KENNEDY
Music by JOHN W. BRATTON

Moderately fast (♩. = 88+)

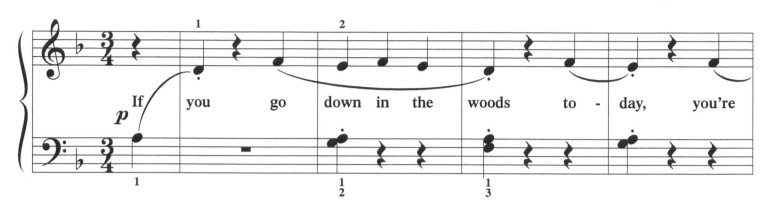

If you go down in the woods to - day, you're

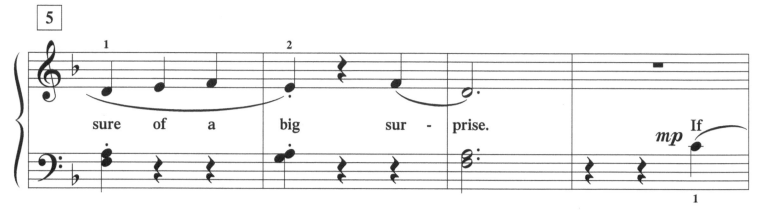

sure of a big sur - prise. If

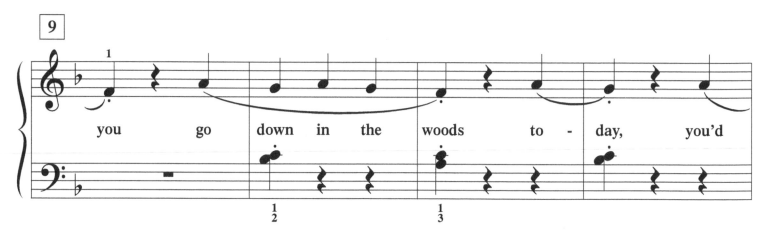

you go down in the woods to - day, you'd

bet - ter go in dis - guise. For

TOUR OF SONGLAND

Take a tour through SongLand by completing each example.

① Connect each Roman Numeral in the cabin to the matching chord.

I   IV   V7

② Circle the rhythm for the opening of *Ding-Dong! The Witch Is Dead.*

③ Write **1 2 3 4** under the correct beats for *Catch a Falling Star.*

④ Write the **key signature** for *New River Train.*

⑤ Decorate the pizza with different musical symbols. (Ex. ♪, ♩, 𝄞, *f*, etc.)

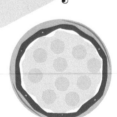

⑥ **Spelling Test.** Put an X through the incorrectly spelled words.

piano	sharp
fortay	kee signature
trouble clef	base clef

⑦ Name the **key signature** for *Oh! Susanna.* Key of ____

⑧ Write the **time signature** for *Happy Birthday.*

Then write your birth date in the blank.

_____